UNIFORMS and GEAR of THE US ARMY SOLDIER

Aurélien MOREL

The Army Combat Uniform

CREW SERVED WEAPONS

OPTICS

TELECOM and PROGRAMS

THE ARMY COMBAT UNIFORM
(ACU)

Since 2008 the Army Combat Uniform has replaced the previous combat uniform of the US Army, the *Battle Dress Uniform* (or BDU). The ACU is fielded in two different patterns, according to the area of deployment: the *Universal Camouflage Pattern* (UCP) and the *Operation Enduring Freedom Camouflage Pattern* (OCP), the latter being a modified version of the Crye Industries Multicam pattern.

Moving away from the BDU concept, the ACU has been developed around the use of body armor,

and as such has Velcro fasteners on the pockets, no lower pockets, the second set of cargo pockets being on the sleeves for easy access when wearing body armor. The vest is also fitted with a straight type collar so the armor is not in contact with the wearer's neck.

The trousers are fitted with 4 cargo pockets: two on the ankles and two on the thighs.

The trousers and shirt are fitted with reinforced knees and elbows that can be fitted with foam protection pads.

Previous page and above.
The ACU corrected a few problems of the old BDU uniform : comfort while wearing body armor, an improved camouflage and a better adaptability to the XXIst Century battlefield.

Left.
OCP-pattern uniform.

The Army Aircrew Combat Uniform
(A2CU)

The *Army Aircrew Combat Uniform* (A2CU) is a two-element flight suit designed for helicopter and light aircraft crews. The A2CU is based on the same concept as the former ABDU (*Aircrew Battle Dress Uniform*) with the use of ACU-type upgrades (straight collar, sleeve pockets, velcros...) and is available in either *Universal Camouflage Pattern* (UCP) or *Operation Enduring Freedom pattern* (OCP).

The A2CU simplifies the use of mission-specific equipment and is an integral part of the Air Warrior program.

Left.
A2CU flight uniform. The similarities with the ACU uniform are easy to spot : general cut, sleeve pockets...

Above.
MH-60 crew wearing the A2CU flight suit.

The Flame Resistant Environmental Ensemble uniform
(FREE)

The *Flame Resistant Environmental Ensemble* is a clothing system designed for helicopter and light aircraft personnel as well as armored vehicles crew. The FREE uniform allows the operator to keep warm while providing a high level of fire protection. It is built as a multi-layer system to adapt to the needs of the user. The FREE is available in both *Universal Camouflage Pattern* (UCP) and *Operation Enduring Freedom Pattern* (OCP).

Right and left.
Fire protection is critical for helicopter and armor crew. With the Flame Resistant Environmental Ensemble, it is combined with weather protection

Army Combat Shirt and Army Combat Pants (ACS & ACP)

The Army Combat Shirt and *Army Combat Pants* are both part of an upgrade program aimed at enhancing combat capabilities for infantry units. Developed from the combat uniforms used by Special Operations soldiers, they boost fire protection and enhance body cooling compared to the ACU. Both are available in either *Universal Camouflage Pattern* (UCP) or *Operation Enduring Freedom Pattern* (OCP).

The ACS is a combat shirt, with the full torso made of Viscose for better cooling when wearing body armor. The camouflaged sleeves are fitted with cargo pockets with Velcro panels, enabling the soldier to wear identification and infrared tags.

The ACP is a set of trousers developed by Crye Industries based on their *Combat Pants*. It reinforced areas (such as the seat or joint areas), and expanding parts on stress zones. Both knees can be fitted with rigid pieces to protect the wearer against hard surfaces (rocks, concrete...). Cargo pockets enhance the carrying ability. Each set of pants are is made with multiple stretching parts to make for an easy fit.

The structure of the Army Combat Shirt (viscose and camouflages twill) makes for better cooling when wearing body armor.

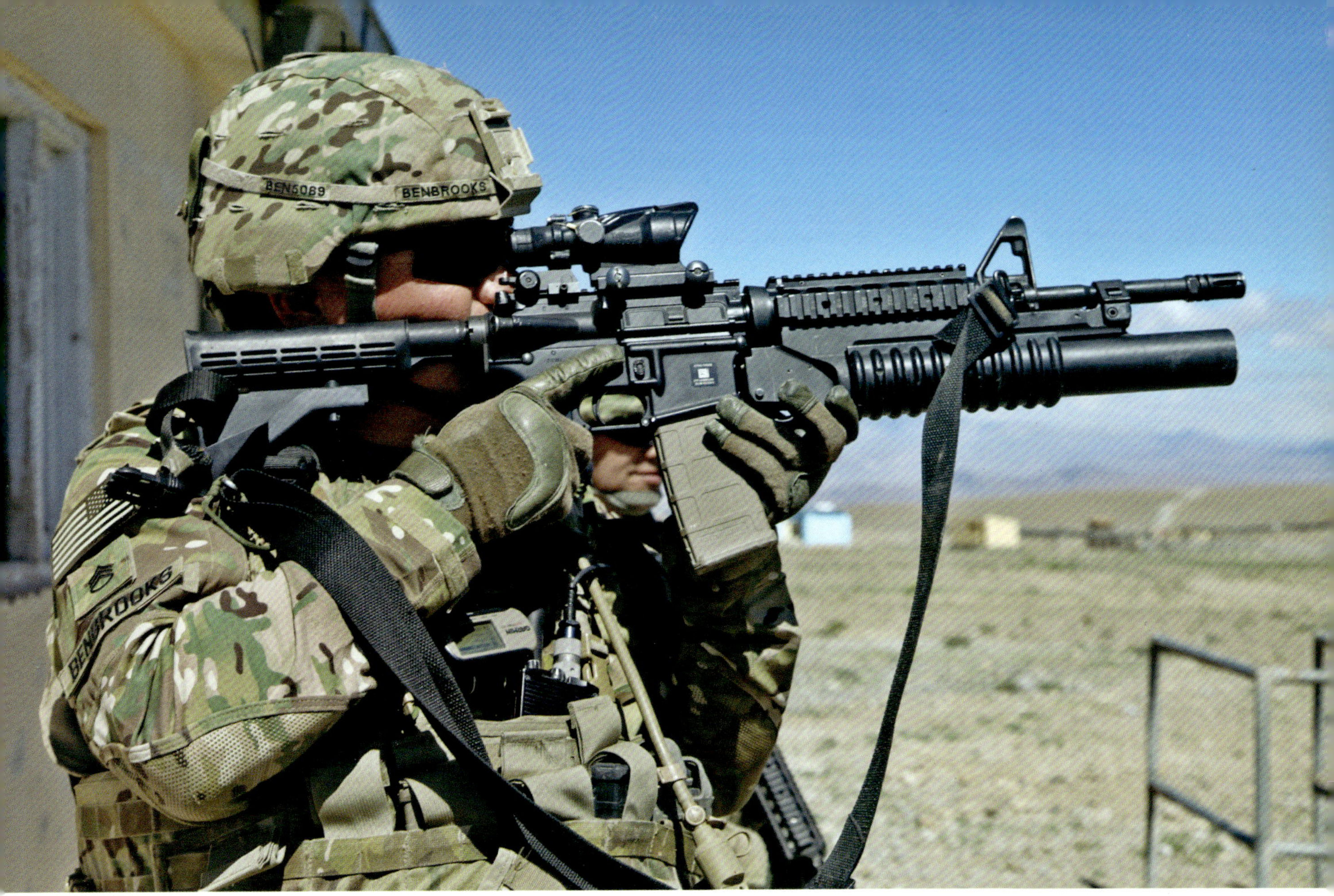
BEN5089
BENBROOKS

ISAF

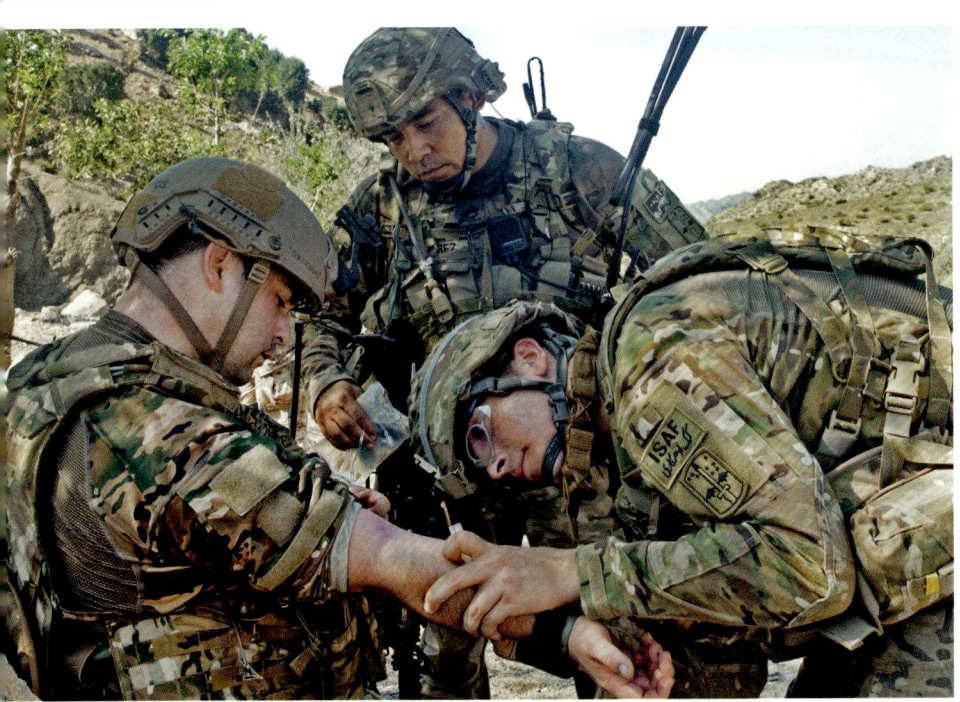

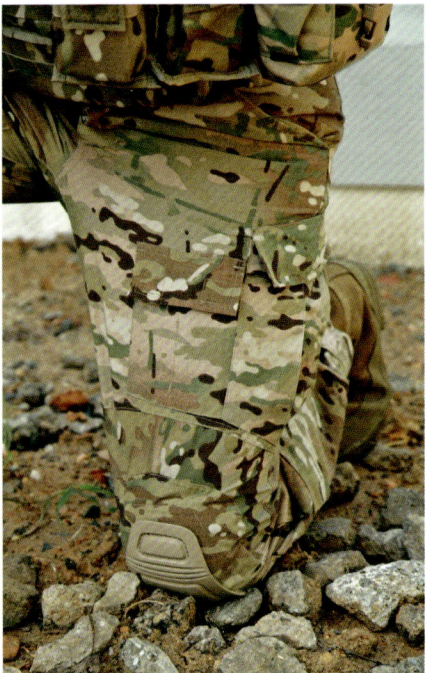

The NRBC JSLIST

(Joint Service Lightweight Integrated Suit Technology)

The *Joint Service Lightweight Integrated Suit Technology* (JSLIST) is a camouflaged chemical and radiological protection suit. It is made of two elements and is worn on the ACU in combat situation. The JSLIST is worn with protection gloves and overboots and a M40 or M50 gas mask. The JSLIST jacket is fitted with an integrated hood that fits around the gas mask for easier use.

The JSLIST is also available as a one-piece overall for armored vehicles crewmen (JC3, JSLIST *Coverall for Combat* Crewmen).

Left.
JSLIST suit worn with protection gloves, overboots and the M50 protection mask.

The Ghillie Suit Accessory Kit Camouflage kit *(GSAK)*

The Ghillie Suit Accessory Kit is an upgrade kit allowing scouts and surveillance units as well as sniper teams to blend in their environment as efficiently as possible. The GSAK is issued as a kit, so the user can assemble the elements in the way most suited to his own use.

The Army Combat Boots
(ACB)

The Army Combat Boot is a lightweight combat boot used in temperate weather. The ACB provides

Left.
Army Combat Boot.

grip in mountainous terrain, good ankle stability and foot protection. The boots are made of hi-grade nylon and are waterproof, fireproof and breathable.

Cold Weather Boots & Specialty Boots
(Cold Weather Boots and Speciality Boots)

The US Army issues four types of cold weather boots: *Extreme Cold Weather Boots* (ECWB), *Intermediate Cold Weather Boots with Removable Liner* (ICWB w/RL), *Modular Boot System* (MBS) and *Modular Combat Boots* (MCB).

The ECWB protects the feet from -5°C to -60°C. It is made of multiple layers of polyester hermetically closed, surrounded by gum, and has a valve for decompression at high altitudes.

The ICWB w/RL is a combat boot for wet cold weather between 0°C and -10°C. The boot is leather with nylon upper, waterproof and breathable.

Left.
mountain Combat Boot.

Right.
Extreme Cold Weather Boot.

Modular Boot System.

The MBS is a multi-use shoe allowing for use from +45°C to -30°C and to be the only combat boot in use in the US Army in the future (every model but the ECWB).

The MCB is a hiking boot focused on boosting the soldier's mobility in rough terrain while providing optimal ankle stability.

Army Combat Boots, HOT WEATHER
(Hot Weather Boots)

The Army Combat Boot – Hot Weather (ACB-HW) is a lightweight combat boot made of leather and light nylon, with built-in grommets for moisture extraction.

The ACB-HW is available with a flame resistant coating (ACB-HW-FR) for crewmen and as a safety version (ACB-HW-ST) with a reinforced sole and a safety steel toe.

The Army Element Fleece
(AEF)

The Army Element Fleece is a cold weather and fireproof fleece for use by light aircraft and helicopter crews. It is made of water repellent fabric and allows the crews to keep warm and dry in operations. The AEF is only made in *Universal Camouflage Pattern* (UCP).

Above.
AEF fleece worn with the LPH hood.

Left.
The Army Element Fleece is worn as the outer shell, directly under the body armor.

The gen III Extended Cold Weather Clothing System
(ECWCS)

The *Extended Cold Weather Clothing System* is a multi-layer isolation system that can be modified to suit the operational needs of servicemen. Each element (layer) can be used alone or in conjunction with other elements of the system. Each element is breathable and allows for optimal cooling, even when wearing body armor. The systems modularity allows soldiers to work from 0°C to -50°C.

The ECWCS gen III is made of 12 elements forming 7 layers: light underwear, extreme cold underwear, fleece, windbreaker, water repellent softshell (pants and jacket), waterproof parka and pants and extreme cold weather pants and parka.

Right.
The different « levels » of the ECWCS system, from left to right : level 3 fleece ; camouflaged level 5 water repellent soft shell ; level 7 extreme low temperatures parka and waterproof pants.

The Modular Sleep System (MSS)

The Modular Sleep System is a multi-layer system made from multiple sleeping bags : the inside is made of the Patrol Bag, a lightweight sleeping bag for temperatures between +2°C and +10°C ; the middle part is made of a heavy duty sleeping bag (-5°C to +2°C) and the exterior is a camouflaged bag. Each part can be used as a separate element or together. When all elements are used in conjunction, it allows protection down to -35°C. The camouflage bag protects against the weather and allows the soldier to blend in the environment. Compression slings allow for easy reduction of the total space when transported. The MSS is also issued with two mats, one in basic foam and one auto-inflating. They allow for good insulation from the ground.

Intermediate Cold Wet Glove and utility gloves *(ICWG)*

The Intermediate Cold Wet Glove is a combat/utility weatherproof glove made for temperatures between -17°C and +5°C, with a lightened insulation at the index finger for ease of use in combat situations. The ICWG can be worn with or without under gloves.

The Combat Glove is a short aramide/leather glove made especially for combat operations. It allows for maximum dexterity while protecting the hands from fire, cuts and other injuries.

The CVC and *Summer Flyers* gloves are lightweight gloves made of Nomex and leather,

Above.
Heavy Duty Gloves

Above.
Heavy Duty Gloves.

Left.
CVC Gloves.

used by crewmen to protect their hands against injuries and burns.

The Men's and Women's Heavy Duty Gloves are heavy leather gloves built for utility work: laying barbed wire, rappelling, fast rope etc.

Left.
Intermediate Cold Wet Glove

The Lightweight Performance Hood
(LPH)

The Lightweight Performance Hood allows the soldier to better protect his/her head from burn injuries. The hood is made of a breathable material and can be worn under the ACH.

Right.
Lightweight Protection Hood worn without a helmet.

19

T-11 parachute, MC-6 parachute below.

The parachutes T-10D, T-11, MC, MFF

The static line-deployed T-10D Parachute is used for combat mass-assault airborne operations and training. Total suspended weight limitation is 360 pounds. The parachute is deployed using either a 15- or 20-foot static line, allowing the parachutist to be delivered by either C-130 or C-17 U.S. Air Force aircraft. The T-10D main parachute is a parabolic shape and has a nominal diameter of 35 feet, 30 suspension lines, and a mesh anti-inversion net. The T-10D Parachute assembly consists of five components: pack tray, troop harness, deployment bag, riser, and canopy.

The MC-6 Maneuverable Canopy Personnel Parachute System offers the airborne Soldier a new tactical, static line deployed, steerable personnel parachute system, replacing the legacy MC-1 series parachute assembly, associated harness, and reserve. The MC-6 has a safer rate of descent, lower opening shock, reduced canopy damage, better turn ratio, and a better glide ratio than the MC1-1C. The system was designed specifically to operate at higher altitudes with heavier weights. These improvements result in better maneuverability, greater canopy control, and reduced jumper injury. This program is a combined U.S. Army and Special Operations Command project.

The Military Free Fall (MFF) Advanced Ram Air Parachute System (ARAPS) provides a multi-mission, high-altitude parachute delivery system that allows personnel to exit at altitudes between 3,500 feet and 35,000 feet. The parachute, which replaces the current MC-4 parachute, supports a total jumper

Above..
T-10D parachutes during a traning exercise.

Left.
The T-11 parachute is scheduled to replace the current T-10D chute..

weight of 450 pounds. It also provides non- MFF personnel with a ram air parachute that is static-line deployed. The ARAPS' three accessory systems are at different stages of the acquisition process:

The Electronic Automatic Activation Device (EAAD) activates and cuts the reserve parachute closing loops if the jumper is falling at 78 mph or faster at the minimum deployment altitude.

The Navigation Aid (NAVAID) will provide in-flight navigation and mission planning capability, allowing parachutists under canopy to locate themselves and the intended drop zone easily. The Parachutist Oxygen Mask (POM) will provide supplemental oxygen at 13,000 feet and higher and will be easier to use and maintain than the current MBU-12P mask.

On this page.
Military Free Fall Chute used by special operations forces.

The Survival Kit, Ready Access, Modular

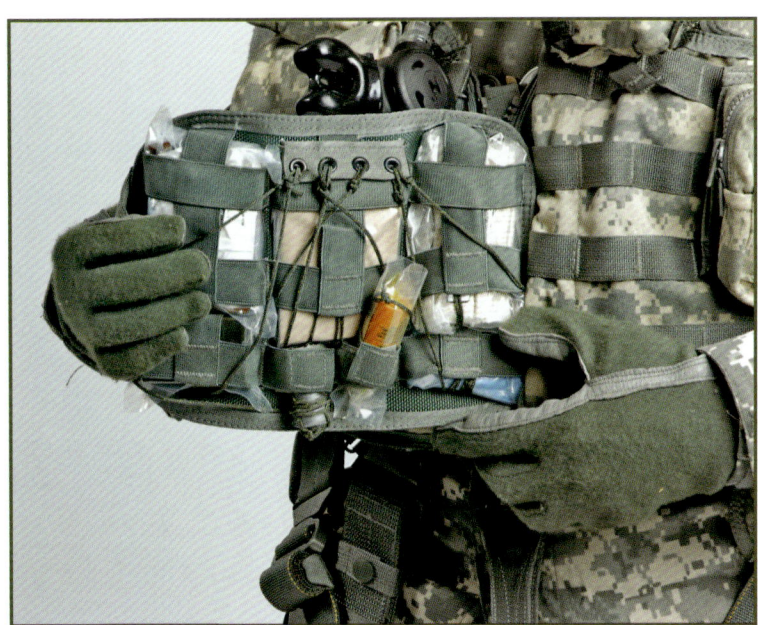

Above.
The insides of the SKRAM bag, with compartments for supplies (water purification systems etc.)

The Survival Kit, Ready Access, Modular is a go-bag type system designed to allow a pilot to survive 72 hours without exterior help. The SKRAM is placed inside the helicopter and is easy to access, to allow use in case of an emergency landing or a crash. The SKRAM can carry rifle ammo, water, food, water purification systems, chlorine tablets and a MSS sleeping bag system.

PROTECTION

The Interceptor Body Armor
(IBA)

The Interceptor Body Armor (IBA) provides the soldier with optimal protection on the battlefield: concussion, fragments, direct and indirect fire. The IBA is designed for high protection and high mobility and allowed since its first generation (fielded in 1997) a significant reduction in life threatening injuries on the battlefield compared to the previous PASGT armor system.

The IBA is made of different elements combined: The IOTV (*Improved Outer Tactical Vest*) is the outer shell and allows the user to operate with the MOLLE system. It serves as the basis of the IBA and protects against fragments and low velocity rounds by using a soft insert. The ESAPI (*Enhanced Small Arms Protective Inserts*) and ESBI (*Enhanced Side Ballistic Insert*), rigid ceramic protections, provide a 360° protection against high-velocity rounds. The IBA can also be fitted with additional parts for the upper arms, groin and collar to extend protection.

Above.
IBA armor system. Above, an ISAF soldier is wearing the IBA armor over an Army Combat Shirt.

The Soldier Plate Carrier System
(SPCS)

On this page.
SPCS plate carrier, planned as a replacement for the IBA system in all situations were mobility is more important than protection.

The Soldier Plate Carrier System is an evolution of the plate carriers used by special operations

forces in Afghanistan since 2001. Issued since 2010, the SPCS is designed to lighten the combat load of soldiers operating in rough (mountainous) terrain by reducing the areas covered (compared to the IBA) while providing a high level of protection with the use of *Enhanced Small Arms Protective Inserts* and *Enhanced Side Ballistic Inserts*. The SPCS is covered with MOLLE-style loops to allow the use of accessory pouches, and has a snap-on system allowing the users to fit a harness for M4 ammunition. The SPCS has a quick-release system in case of immediate danger (drowning...).

The Advanced Bomb Suit

(ABS)

The Advanced Bomb Suit is an Explosive Ordnance Disposal suit designed for optimal 360° protection against explosions and shrapnel. The suit is also fire-resistant.

The ABS also has a passive cooling system, using ice to improve comfort over time.

Every part of the suit is modular to allow the users to adapt to their mission and environment, and the suit has been designed with provisions for enhancements in protection and communication.

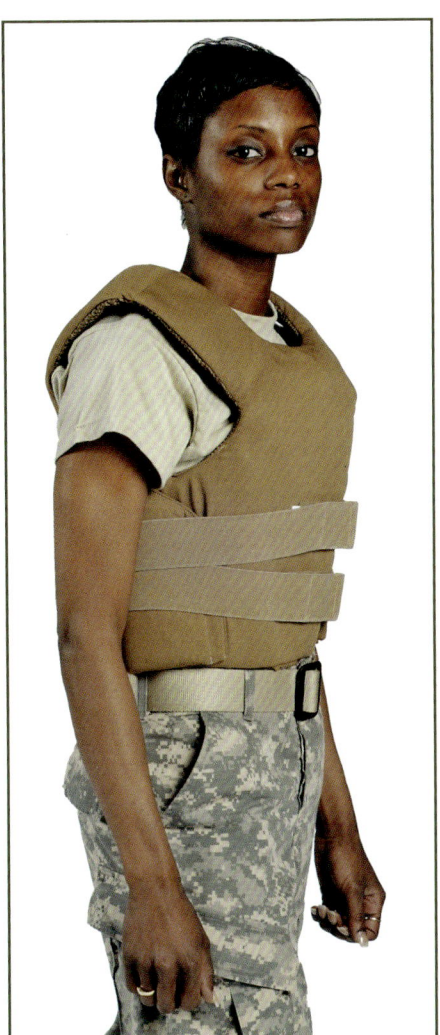

The Concealable Body Armor
(CBA)

The Concealable Body Armors are designed for use by military police, investigation services (CID) and correction officers. They allow for ballistic and stabbing protection while being low-key enough to be concealed under civilian clothing. The CBA are an off-the-shelf product but are to be replaced by a single US Army specific model as of late 2012.

Above.
CBA models

Individual Soldier Hydration

The individual hydration system is divided in multiple elements: the 1 quart rigid canteen; the 2 quart bladder canteen; the Cold Weather Canteen System, an insulated canteen for use down to -40°C; *the MOLLE hydration system*, bladder backpack-type system that can be used alone or mounted on the IBA our SPCS. Every one of those systems is compatible with CRBN equipment and can be connected to the M40 and M50 gas masks. Every soldier is also issued *Individual Water Treatment Devices,* purification systems to allow use of local water sources.

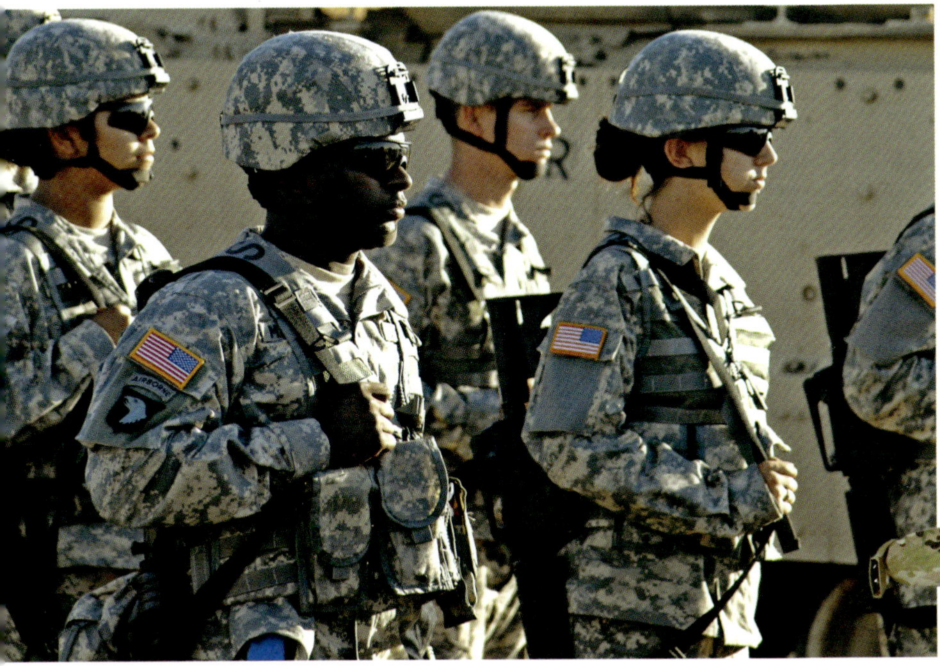

Below.
MOLLE system medium ruck.

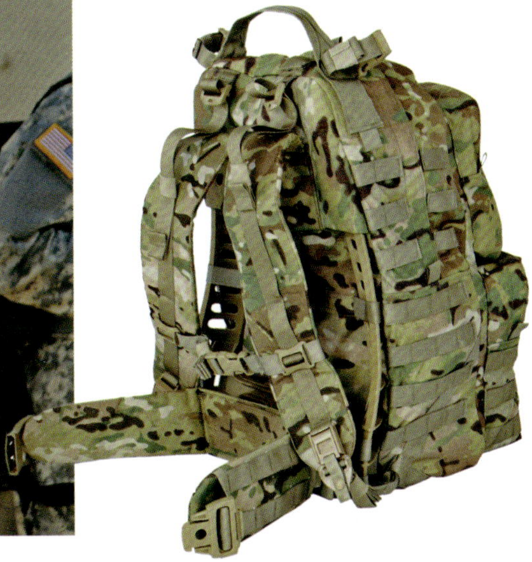

The Modular Lightweight Load carrying Equipment system *(MOLLE)*

The MOLLE system is a modular carrying system that allows the soldier to adapt his carrying setup to the mission at hands and his personal preferences. The basic Rifleman kit contains a *Tactical Assault Panel* (TAP) that carries 6 rifle magazines and a MBITR radio or GPS device. Loops on the TAP allow for the use of other accessory pouches provided in the kit for weapons or accessories (pistol, knife, magazines, grenades...). *The Rifleman kit* is also provided with an *Assault Pack* (*light backpack*), a *Medium Ruck* and a *Large Rucksack*. Specialists kits are also available in the MOLLE range: *Grenadier* (40 mm rounds), *Medic* (medical kits) and *Squad Automatic Weapon* (pouches for SAW ammunition belts).

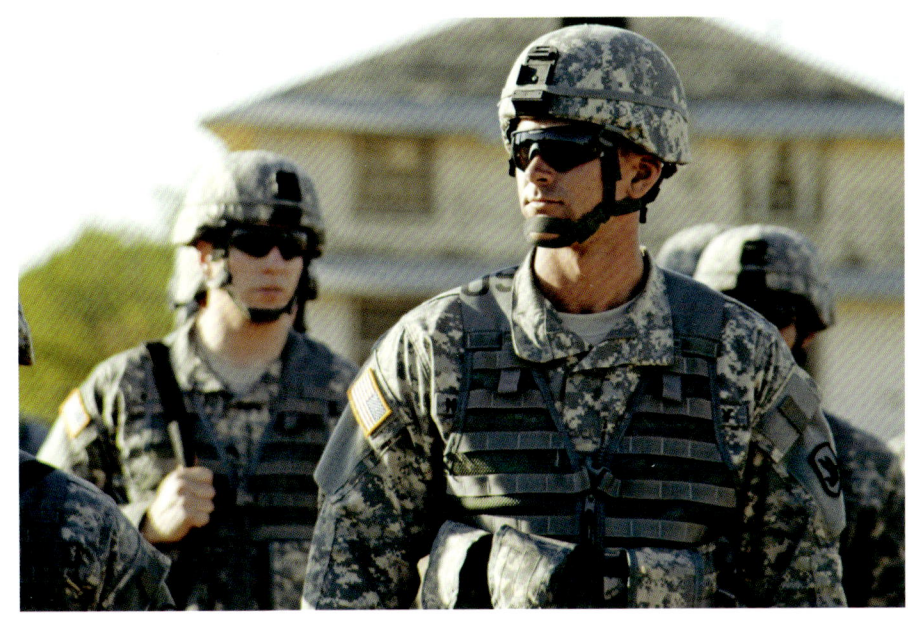

The Advanced Combat Helmet

(ACH)

The *Advanced Combat Helmet* is a modular helmet based on the MICH system (*Modular Integrated Communications Helmet*) used by special operation forces. The ACH is lighter, more resistant and more mission-adaptable than the former *US Army helmet,* the PASGT.

The ACH uses a pad system (memory foam) to perfectly fit the head of the soldier and enhance the protection against concussions. The strap is 4-point, which enhances stability and comfort.

The ACH can be used with all the communication and night vision devices used by the US Army (ANVIS, AN/PVS-14, AN/PSQ-20) and can be fitted with a ballistic neck pad to cover the space between the IBA collar and the bottom of the helmet.

Left.
ACH helmet with the UCP cover. The nylon loops stops ballistic goggles from moving around.

The Combat Vehicle Crewman Helmet *(CV H)*

The *Combat Vehicle Crewman Helmet* (CVCH) is a non-modular helmet with integrated communication capabilities developed for use by armored carriers and battle tanks personnel (M1 Abrams, M3 Bradley…) for individual ballistic protection. The CVCH is equipped with a system allowing connection to any NATO type intercom while providing acoustic protection.

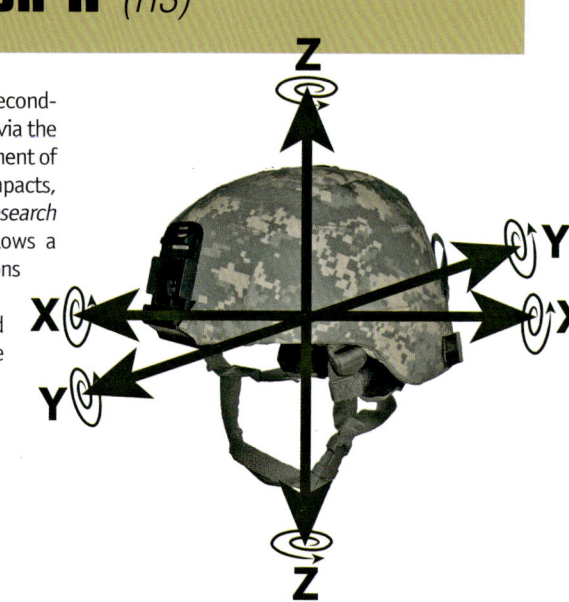

HELMET SENSORS Gen II *(HS)*

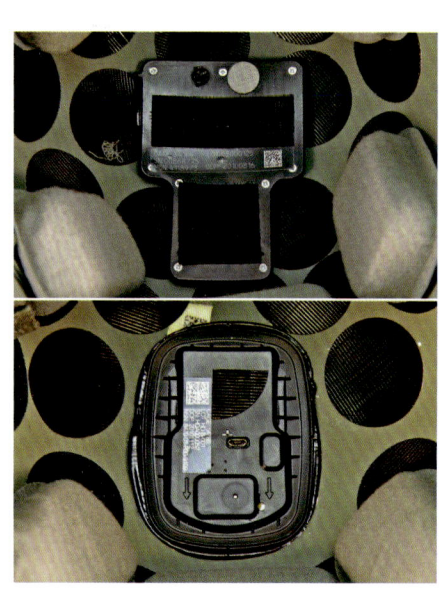

The *Helmet Sensor* (HS) system is a second-generation sensor allowing the recording, via the *Data Retrieval System* (DRS), of any movement of the helmet and the head. In case of hard impacts, the information is sent to the *Medical Research and Material Command* (MRCM) and allows a better care for injuries related to explosions and high velocity impacts.

The *HS system* is a simple sensor placed inside the helmet with wireless or wire connection depending on the hardware.

The Military Combat Eye Protections
(MCEP)

The MCEP system is made of a number of ballistic masks and goggles used by the US Army for combat operations.

Both types of hardware are designed to protect the eyes of the soldier against shrapnel, UV rays, lasers, dust and wind. This reduces the occurrence of eye damage both on the battlefield and in training.

The MCEP program permits to qualify commercial off-the-shelf products following the ANSI Z87.1 and durability criteria.

Both types of systems (goggles and masks) can be modified by adding correction lenses and tinted lenses.

Above.
Ballistic goggles stemming from the MCEP program, worn with complete tactical gear.

Above.
Ballistic glasses stemming from the MCEP program.

The Aircrew Integrated Helmet System
HGU-56/P *(AIHS)*

The *HGU-56/P Aircrew Integrated Helmet System* is the standard helmet for helicopter crews in the US Army. Replacing the SPH-4, the HGU-56/P is 15% lighter and offers better protection from shrapnel and hits. The HGU-56/P can also be fitted with an additional maxillofacial shield for added forward protection.

The Apache Aircrew Integrated Helmet
(AAIH)

The *Apache Aircrew Integrated Helmet* (AAIH) is a new helmet designed to allow AH-64D Apache Block III to maximize performance of their helicopter via a brand new user interface.

INDIVIDUAL ARMAMENT AND ACCESSORIES

The US M9 Pistol

The M9 is a double action semi automatic pistol introduced to active service in 1985. It shoots 9X19mm Parabellum ammo (NATO standard caliber) and is fed from a 15 rounds magazine.

A railed adapter allows the use of an ILWLP module, allowing the M9 to be more efficient in low-light conditions.

The M4 and M4A1 Carbines

The M4 and M4A1 Carbines are the most widely used weapons in the US Army. A shortened version of the M16 rifle, the M4 Carbine is a compact and versatile weapon and allows users to engage protected and unprotected targets in any situation, and it is well suited for urban combat operations. The M4A1 carbine is an automatic version of the M4.

Both models can be fitted with the M203 and M320 grenade launchers and with the secondary M26 MASS shotgun.

In 2011, the US Army launched two carbine programs with two objectives: either upgrading the M4 or replacing it with an entirely new platform.

Since 2010, a 3rd generation magazine is available for the M4. Those new improved magazines can be identified by their khaki follower.

The M16A2 et M16A4 rifles

The M16 rifle has been in US Army service since 1965 and is currently manufactured under the M16A4 designation. The US Army currently fields two variants of the rifle: The M16A2, with fixed carry handle and sights and most of the time a plastic handguard, and the M16A4, with removable carry handle allowing for easy use of optics and most of the time fitted with the *M5 Adapter Rail System* that allows users to fit accessories (lights, lasers, GLI...).

Every variant of the M16 can be fitted with the M203 and M320 grenade launchers.

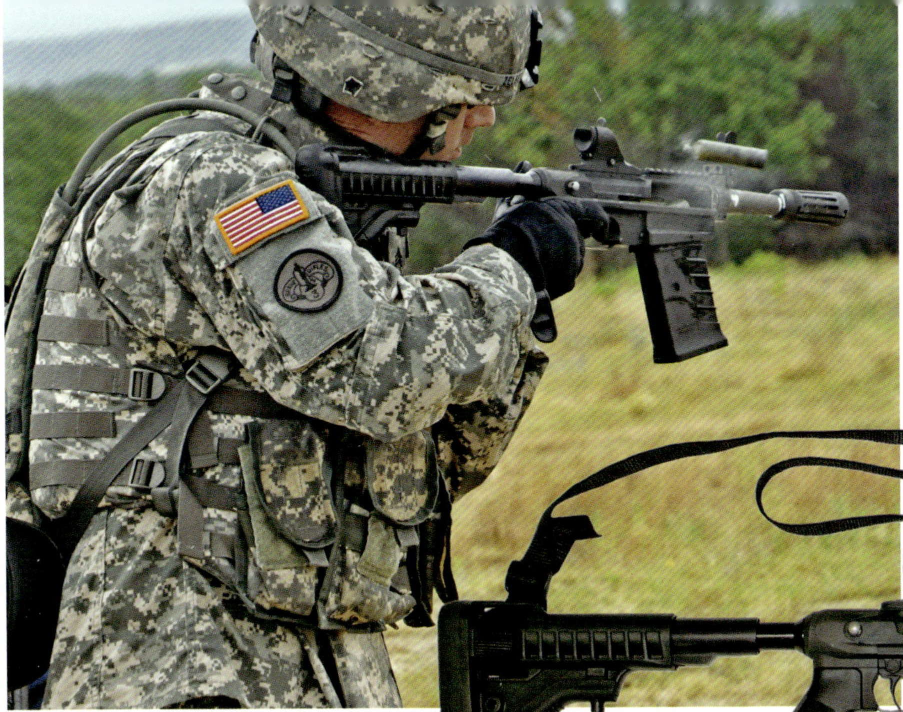

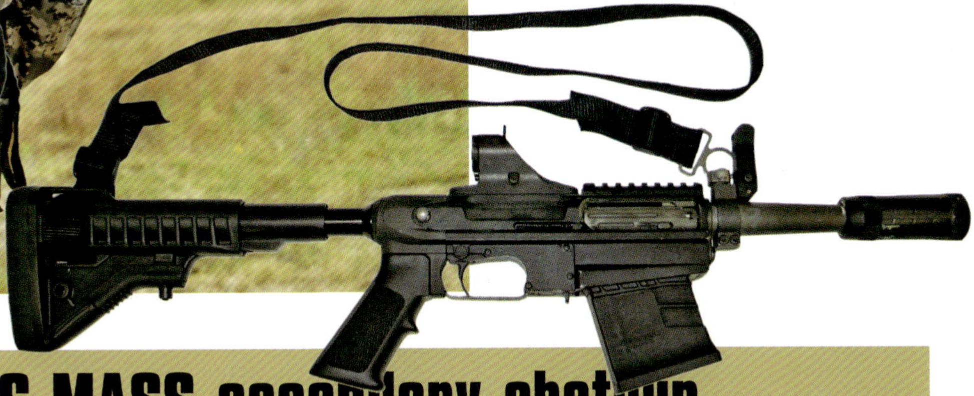

Left and bellow.
The M26 MASS shotgun can be used independently from the M4 Carbine by adding a pistol grip or a stock, both delivered with the M26 kit. This allows for a less bulky weapon when carrying a carbine is not necessary.

The M26 MASS secondary shotgun

The *M26 Modular Accessory Shotgun System* (MASS) is a straight-pull bolt-action shotgun in 12 gauge and is fed from a box magazine. The MASS can be used as an independent weapon or fitted under the M4 Carbine. This allows the user to switch between rifle and shotgun with ease and very fast.

The straight-pull action allows for the use of less-lethal rounds.

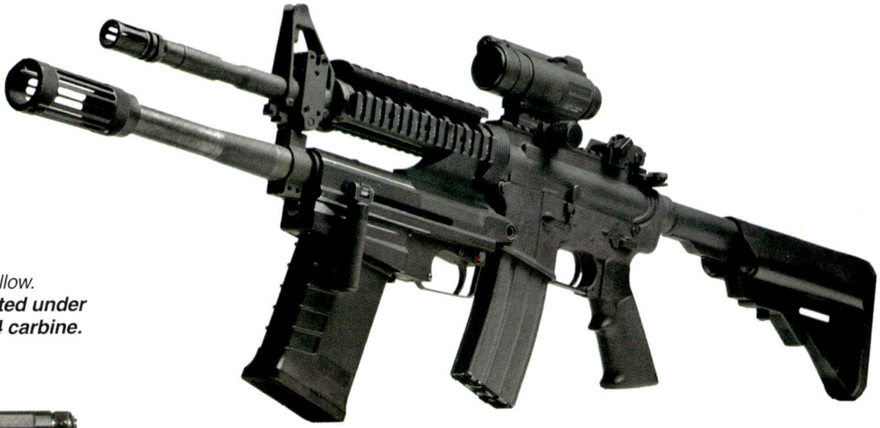

Right and bellow.
M26 MASS mounted under the barrel of a M4 carbine.

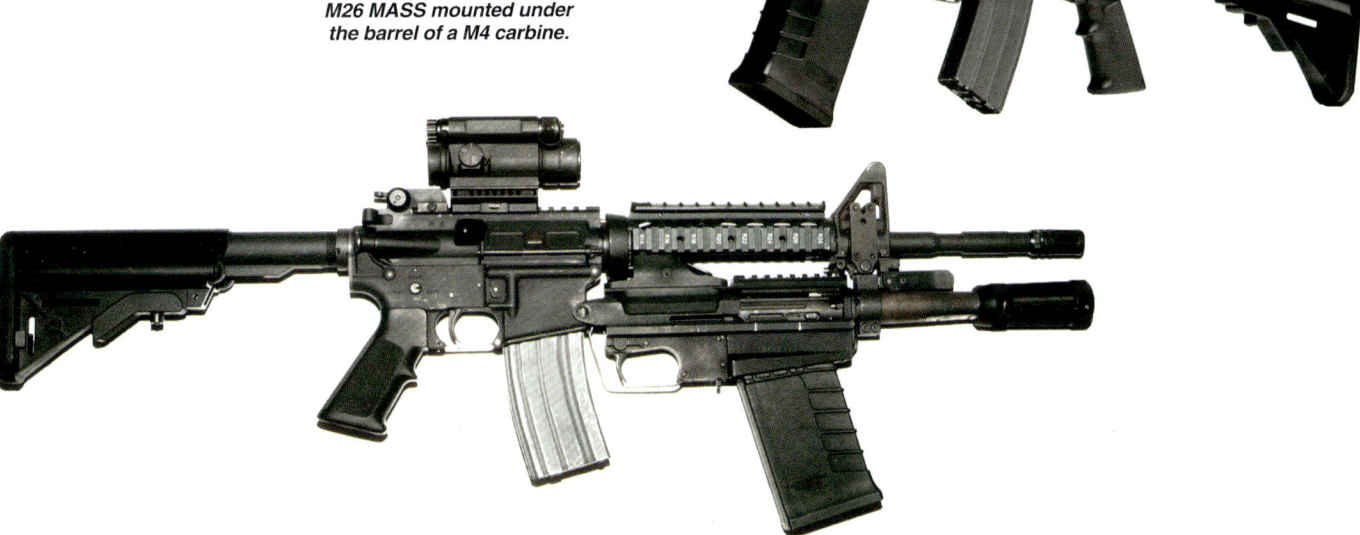

Above and bellow.
The M590 shotgun is often used by entry teams to break locks and open doors.

The M590 pump action shotgun

The M590 is a pump action shotgun developed by Mossberg on the basis of their M500 hunting shotgun. It's an effective short-range weapon and can be loaded with lethal or less-lethal rounds depending on the mission. M590s are mostly issued to military police and entry teams.

Left and bellow.
M590 pump action shotgun with and without ghost ring sights.

The M24 SWS rifle
(SWS)

The *M24 Sniper Weapon System* is a bolt-action precision rifle firing 7.62mm NATO rounds. It is built to engage targets up to 800 meters. The M24 is being gradually replaced by the semi-automatic M110 SASS, and some M24 SWS are being upgraded to the .300 WM chambered XM2010 standard.

Above and left.
The M24 SMS rifle has been used by US Army sniper teams since the 1980s. It is fitted here with a day/night vision PVS-10 scope (top) and a Leupold Mk4 day scope (bottom).

Right and bellow.
M107 LRSR fitted with different optics.

The M107 Long Range Sniper Rifle *(LRSR)*

The *M107* is a semi automatic sniper rifle built on the basis of the Barrett M82. With its .50 BMG ammunition, it is able to engage targets up to 2000 meters. The M107 is fed from a 10 rounds magazine and can be used with a wide variety of optics and accessories due to its rails.

The M107s long range makes it a weapon well suited to hunt down other snipers while staying out of their range. The M107 LRSR is also used by EOD teams to trigger IEDs from a distance.

The M110 SASS Semi Auto Sniper Rifle *(SASS)*

The *M110 Semi Auto Sniper System* is a semi automatic rifle in 7.62mm NATO built to engage multiple targets between 500 and 800 meters faster than the previous bolt action sniper rifles (M24 SWS). The M110 can be used with every accessory issued by the US Army due to its rail interface. It has been designed to be used with a specific sound suppressor.

The M14 EBR *(Enhanced Battle Rifle)*

The *M14 Enhanced Battle Rifle* (EBR) is an evolution of the 1960s M14 battle rifle used by the US Army in Vietnam. The EBR rifle is fitted with an aluminum chassis equipped with rails for accessories and a retracting stock that can be fitted to the user. The M14 EBR has been issued in Afghanistan to fill the gap between the M4 carbine and sniper rifles on the battlefield (need for a medium-range semi-automatic battle rifle). The M14 is being replaced by the M110 SASS.

The M320 Grenade Launcher

The M320 is a one-shot grenade launcher built by Heckler & Koch and based on the AG36. It can be fitted on the M4 carbine and M16 rifle or be used alone.

The M320 is loaded by tilting the barrel to the side. This allows the use of any 40mm cartridge with no limit regarding length. The safety is provided by a double action trigger, allowing hitting the primer a second time if at the first shot the grenade did not go off.

Right.
Soldier armed with a M4 carbine fitted with the M320 grenade launcher.

Left.
M320 in two configurations : fitted under the M4 carbine (top) **and as a stand-alone with stock** (bottom).

The M203A2 Grenade Launcher

The M203A2 grenade launcher is the latest evolution of the M203 launcher. It is a one-shot 40mm grenade launcher that can be fitted to any M16 rifle or M4 carbine. The M203 can be used with either a mechanical sight or a *Day/Night Sight* (DNS) to allow better shot placement.

The M203 launcher is being replaced by the M320.

Above and bellow.
The M203 has only slightly evolved since its introduction in the 1970s. However, the few last years have seen the introduction of hi-tech aiming devices to reduce collateral damage.

The XM25 ISAAS Semi Automatic Launcher
(Individual Semi Automatic Airburst System)

The *XM25 Individual Semi-Automatic Airburst System* (ISAAS) enables the small unit and individual Soldier to engage defilade targets by providing a 25mm air bursting capability that can be used in all operational environments. The ISAAS is an individually fired, semi-automatic, man-portable weapon system. An individual Soldier employing basic rifle marksmanship skills can effectively engage exposed or defilade targets in just seconds out to 700 meters. The system allows the individual Soldier to quickly and accurately engage targets by producing an adjusted aim point based on range, environmental factors, and user inputs. The target acquisition/fire control integrates thermal capability with direct view optics, laser rangefinder, compass, fuse setter, ballistic computer, and an internal display.

51

The CQB Accessories Kit
(Close Quarters Battle)

The *CQB* kit is made of several accessories allowing the M4 Carbine to be more modular: Adapter Rail System handguard with rails, bipod for precision shooting, a vertical grip/pod, a tactical 3-point sling, an enhanced cleaning kit.

Left.
Basic CQB kit for the M4 carbine.

MFAL Lights Family
(MultiFunction Aiming Lights)

The *Multifunction Aiming Lights* (MFAL) family has two components: the *AN/PEQ-15 Advanced Target Pointer Illuminator Aiming Light* (ATPIAL) and the AN/PEQ-15A *Dual Beam Aiming Laser – Advanced²* (DBAL-A²). The MFAL provide any weapon fitted with NATO rails with upgraded day/night targeting abilities. Each unit has a visible laser pointer, a focused beam infrared laser pointer, and a variable beam laser pointer. They can be used mounted on a gun or alone.

AN/PEQ-15A.

AN/PEQ-15.

The ILWLP AN/PEQ-14 module
(Integrated Laser White Light Pointer)

The *AN/PEQ-14 Integrated Laser White Light Pointer* (ILWLP) is a lamp/laser module that can be used alone or fitted to a handgun via a rail mount. The ILWLP is mainly used by military police on the M9 pistol. The ILWLP has a white visible light, a visible laser pointer and an infrared laser pointer. They can be used at the same time or independently.

The Individual Gunshot Detector
(IGD)

The *Individual Gunshot Detector* (IGD) is a passive acoustic system allowing the troops to locate the point of origin of a gunshot. The system is able to give the location of a gunshot with margins of error of 15% on the angle and 20% on the distance, and makes locating sniper easier for the troops.

The WML and CSWL Tactical Lights
(Weapon Mounted Light et Crew served Weapon Light)

The *Weapon Mounted Light* (WML) and *Crew Served Weapon Light* (CSWL) are weapon-mounted tactical lights. They allow soldiers to get better target sights in low light conditions. The WML is to be fitted to a NATO/mil-std-1913 rail on a rifle (M16), carbine (M4) or light/medium machine gun (M249, M240) and has a practical range of 20 meters. The CSWL is to be fitted to a heavy crew served weapon (M2HB, Mk19...) and has a 50 watt HID light.

Above.
WML Tactical Weapon Light

CSWL mounted on the Mk19 GMG.

CSWL mounted on the M2 HMG.

The GLIS interdiction lasers
(Green Laser Interdiction System)

The *Green Laser Interdiction System* (GLIS) is a non-lethal weapon mounted laser designed for interdiction. The laser is powerful enough to be inconvenient to humans without any harm. It can be used to stop a hostile action or civilians from going into an active combat zone.

Left.
The GLIS devices are available in multiple versions depending on the weapon they are fitted to.

The ALP LA-8/P Laser Pointer

(Aircrew Laser Pointer)

The *Aircrew Laser Pointer* (ALP) LA-8/P is a glove-mounted system made for target acquisition and *Identification Friend or Foe* (IFF).

Bellow.
Hands Free Helmet-Mounted Light.

Individual Lights

The soldier is issued a number of individual lights: the *Hands-Free helmet-mounted Light* (HFHL) to fit on the ACH or IBA, and the *Hand Held Tactical Light* (HHTL) for work or research.

Bellow, left.
Hand Held Tactical Light.

Ci-dessous.
Hand Held Tactical Light.

CREW SERVED WEAPONS

The M249 SAW

(Squad Automatic Weapon)

The *M249 Squad Automatic Weapon* is a light machine gun fed from a box magazine or a belt, chambered for 5.56 NATO SS109 ammo. It was designed for fire support at the fire team level and offers a rate of fire superior to that of the M4 and M16. The latest upgrades fielded shorter barrels and M4-style retracting stock, making it a better tool for close quarters combat.

Right.
The latest version of the M249 SAW, complete with short barrel and retractable stock.

The M240 machine gun

(Light Machine Gun)

The M240 is a 7.62mm NATO, belt-fed medium machine gun based on the FN MAG and widely used by the US military in 3 variants:

The M240B is the standard ground weapon, used by foot soldiers and mounted on armored carriers and tanks for close-quarter self defense.

The M240H is the defensive version used on helicopters. It is issued with a modification kit for use on the ground.

The M240L is the lightweight version of the M240B. Made with a titanium receiver, the M240L loses 2.5kg compared to the 240B when using a short barrel. The ergonomics of the 240L are also improved by the use of a retractable stock.

Bellow.
A M240L, equipped with a short barrel, a retractable stock and the M145 MGO optic.

The M2 Heavy Machine Gun
(Machine Gun)

The M2 is a crew-served, belt fed heavy machine gun chambered for the .50" BMG round. The M2 is very efficient against infantry, light trucks and low-flying aircrafts. The M2 can be mounted on armored or unarmored vehicles and be used on strongpoints. The M2 provides heavy firepower up to 1800 meters.

The M2A1 is an improved version of the M2, using a quick-change barrel for an improved cyclic rate of fire, upgraded internals for reliability and a muzzle break to reduce the visual signature.

The XM806 Heavy Machine Gun

(Machine Gun)

The XM806 heavy machine gun is a replacement for the M2 machine gun. The XM806 is lighter (by half) and easier to move around the battlefield. The XM806 is belt fed and runs on the same .50" BMG ammo as the M2.

Bellow.
Still, the XM806 is supposed to replace some of the M2s in a few years.

The M153 CROWS

(Common Remotely Operated Weapon Station)

The *M153 Common Remotely Operated Weapon Station* (CROWS) is a remote operated turret and can be fitted with any US Army crew operated weapon (M2, Mk19, M240, and M249).
The CROWS turret is piloted from inside the vehicle and provides the user with day/night and thermal imaging. Equipped with a range finder, the CROWS can automatically correct the ballistics of the weapon and can scan and automatically suppress targets on a designated quadrant.

The Mk19 GMG automatic grenade launcher
(Grenade Machine Gun)

The *Mk19 Grenade Machine Gun* (GMG) is a belt-fed 40mm automatic grenade launcher. The Mk19 can be fitted to a vehicle, a strongpoint or a CROWS system. The Mk19 allows the engagement of light trucks and strongpoints with more firepower than the M2.

OPTICS

The M150 Rifle Combat Optic

The *M150 RCO* is an all-weather battery-free combat optic with 4x magnification that provides medium-range capability to the M4 and M16 weapons systems. The M150 uses a tritium-powered system to provide an illuminated reticule in low-light conditions.

The M145 Machine Gun Optic

The *M145 Machine Gun Optic* (MGO) is a combat optic with a 3.4 magnification, issued for use with the M240 and 249 machine guns. The use of the M145 enhances chances to hit a standing target at medium range.

the M68 Close Combat Optic

The *M68 Close Combat Optic* (CCO) is a red dot optic with no magnification made for fast targeting at short ranges. The M68 allows the shooter to use its weapons with both eyes opened, enhancing the field of vision and the response to peripheral threats. The M68 CCO can be mounted on any weapon with built-in mil-std-1913 accessory rail and can be used for up to 300 meters.

The STORM MLRF AN/PSQ-23 system
(Small Tactical Optical Rifle Mounted, Micro-Laser Range Finder)

The *STORM AN/PSQ-23 Micro-Laser RangeFinder* is a rifle module with range finding, GPS tracking, visible/infrared laser and digital compass functionalities. The STORM allows the foot soldier to locate targets and check their distance, making it easier to use their individual or collective weapons.

The AN/PAS-13 Thermal Weapon Sight
(Thermal Weapon Sight)

The *AN/PAS-13 Thermal Weapon Sight* (TWS) is an all-weather thermal optic sight that can be used with any weapon provided they are fitted with a mil-std-1913 rail. The TWS allows for the shooter to see targets through obscurants (fog, darkness, rain…) and is available in three versions depending on the weapon used : *AN/PAS-13(V)1 Light Weapon Thermal Sight*, for rifles (M4 et M16) ; *AN/PAS-13(V)2 Medium Weapon Thermal Sight, machine guns* (M249, M240) ; *AN/PAS-13(V)3 Heavy Weapon Thermal Sight*, providing thermal and magnification for long range weapons (M2HB, Mk19, M24, M107).

The (Clip On SNS) AN/PVS-30 night vision sight
(Sniper Night Sight)

The *AN/PVS-30 SNS* (Sniper Night Sight) is a night vision scope designed to be used in conjunction with a day-time optic on sniper rifles like the M110 SASS or the XM2010. The PVS-30 amplifies residual light and allows target identification up to 600 meters. The PVS-30 is placed in front of the day optic, and allows the user to keep the original zero on his scope.

The M22, M24, M25 binoculars

The M22 are combat binoculars with a 7x magnification allowing for target identification up to 1000 meters. The M22s are standard issue in the US Army under the *"field binoculars"* name.

The M24 binoculars are a more compact (around 80%), lighter (around 50%) alternative to the M22.

The M25 binoculars are a stabilized optical system providing a 14x magnification. The M25s allow for target identification at ranges up to 4000 meters and can be used in conjunction with light amplification optics for night time use.

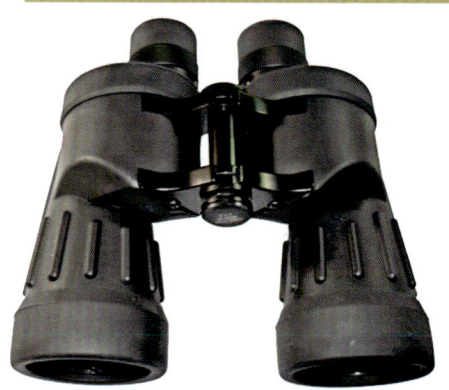

M22.

M25.

M24

The M151 monocular

The M151 monocular is a spotter scope allowing for target identification at long range. The scope has a mildot reticle so the spotter can easily calculate elevations and distance as well as other important information and communicate them to the shooter. The scope has a 12 to 40x magnification.

An AN/PVS-14 monocular can be fitted to the M151 for night-vision capabilities.

The ENVG AN/PSQ-20 night vision monocular

(Enhanced Night Vision Goggle)

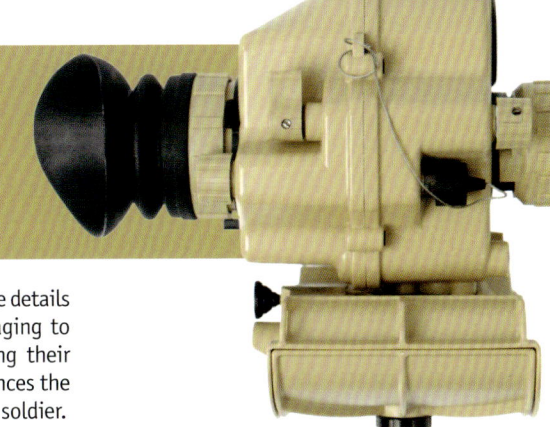

The *AN/PSQ-20 Enhanced Night Vision Goggle* (ENVG) is a combination of several night vision devices: light amplification (active and passive) and thermal imaging. The use of those two systems allows the user to use both the infrared imaging to move around and see details of the landscape and the thermal imaging to track targets through obscurants using their heat signature. The ENVG greatly enhances the target acquisition abilities of the foot soldier.

the MNVD AN/PVS-14 night vision monocular

(Monocular Night Vision Device)

The *AN/PVS-14 Monocular Night Vision Device* is a stand-alone monocular built around a 3rd generation light amplification system.

The PVS-14 can be used alone or mounted on a helmet, or on a rifle in conjunction with a day-time scope to enhance night-time combat abilities.

69

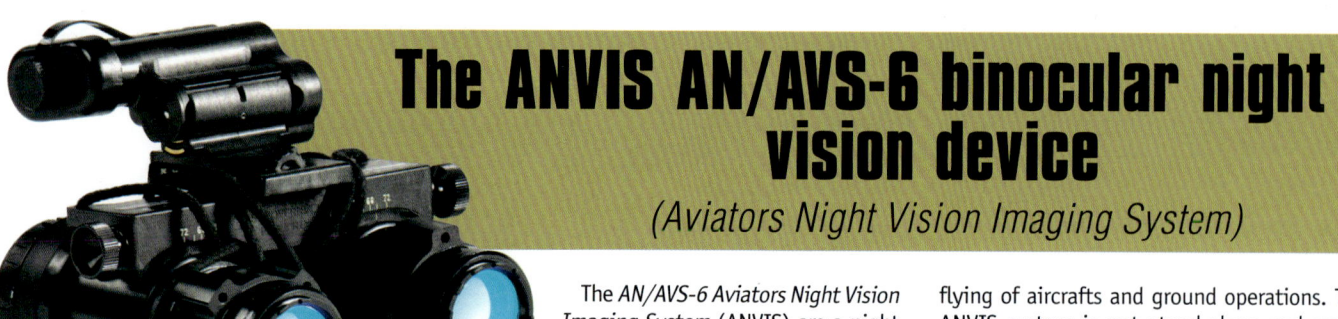

The ANVIS AN/AVS-6 binocular night vision device

(Aviators Night Vision Imaging System)

The *AN/AVS-6 Aviators Night Vision Imaging System* (ANVIS) are a night vision binocular system using 3rd generation light amplification system. The use of a binocular system allows the user to keep his 3D vision and facilitates the flying of aircrafts and ground operations. The ANVIS system is not stand-alone and needs a power source to work. The binoculars are powered through a helmet mount and the power is provided either by a battery pack or the electrical system of a helicopter.

The STTW AN/PPS-26 tracking system

(Sense Through The Wall)

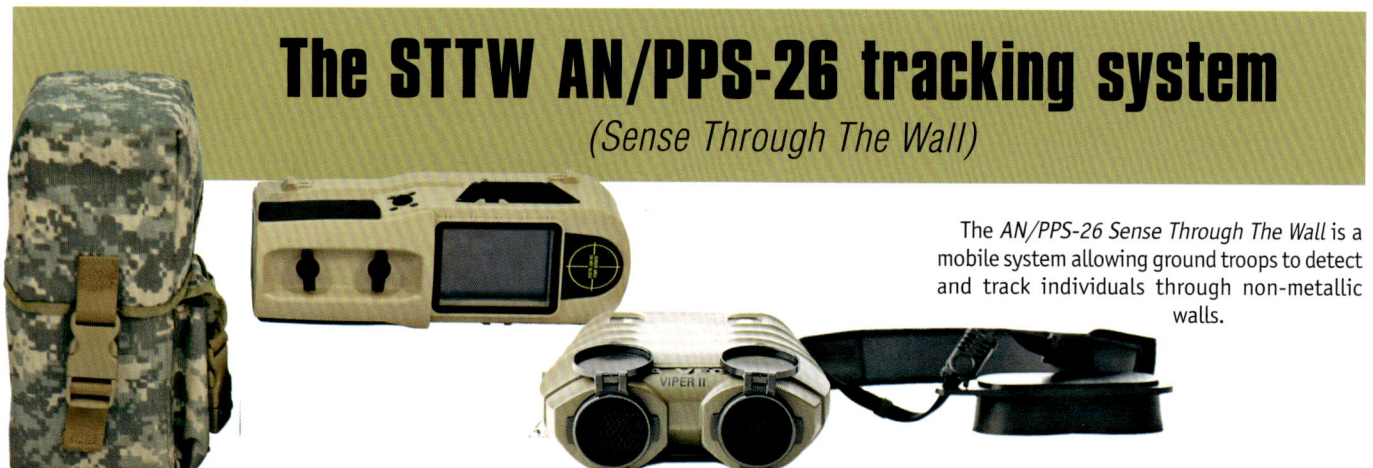

The *AN/PPS-26 Sense Through The Wall* is a mobile system allowing ground troops to detect and track individuals through non-metallic walls.

The LTL targeting systems

(Laser Target Locator)

The *Laser Target Locator* (LTL) family is made of three light off-the-shelf laser target designators bought to fill a gap in the Army's arsenal: The Vector 21, the Mark VII/VIIE and the TRIGR. Each of those can be used to tag a target, either using a laser to 'paint' the target or by uploading the GPS coordinates to the fire base.

The LLDR AN/PED-1 target designator
(Lightweight Laser Designator Rangefinder)

The *AN/PED-1 Lightweight Laser Designator Rangefinder* (LLDR) is a man-portable laser targeting system designed to allow infantry to 'paint' targets for air support or artillery. The basic optical system has a thermal sensor, a laser rangefinder, an electronic compass, a laser marker and an integrated GPS module able to export information to fire support bases.

The system can break down in two modules that can be used independently, the Target Locator Module (TLM) and the *Laser Designator module* (LDM).

Left.
Complete AN/PED-1: TLM (lower part) and LDM (upper part).

The JETS targeting system
(Joint Effects Targeting System)

The *Joint Effects Targeting System* (JETS) is a joint effort between the US Army and US Air Force to provide a lightweight one-man operated targeting system for ground troops. The JETS system breaks down in two parts: the TLDS (*Target Location Designation System*) locates and tags the target, and the TECS (*Target Effects Coordination System*) sends the information on the battle network, allowing any soldier to locate the target.

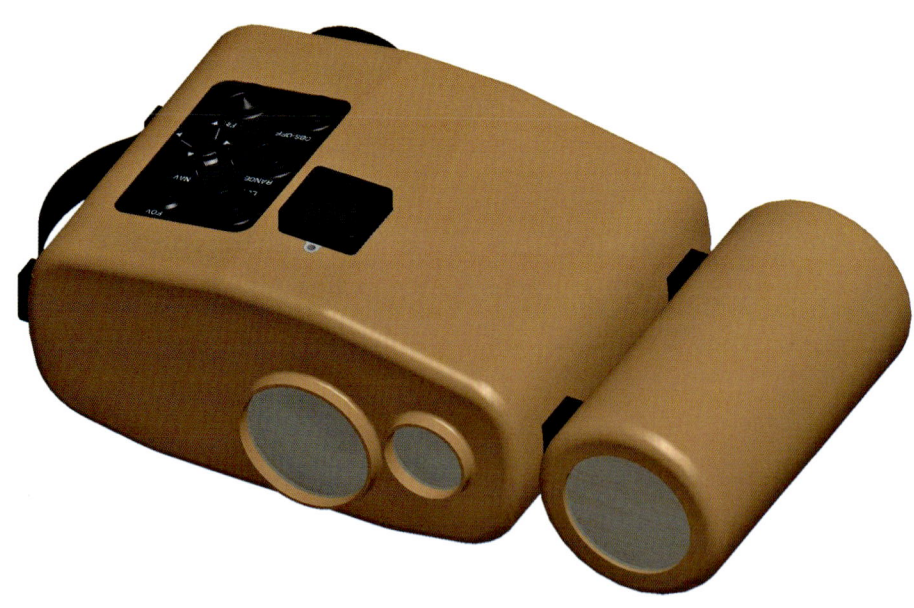

the AN/AVS-7 heads up display

The *AN/AVS-7 Heads Up Display* (HUD) is a heads up interface based on the ANVIS AVS-6 binoculars allowing pilots to display pertinent flight information directly onto their night vision goggles. This reduces the need to check the instruments and stay aware of the surroundings of the aircraft at all times.

Above.
Complete AN/AVS-7 system, with NVGs, display system (heads up display) and connexion to the helicopter's avionics.

Left.
NA/AVS-7 on a HGU-56/P helmet. One can easily spot the proximity with the ANVIS night vision system.

TELECOM and PROGRAMS

the EDM tablet
(Electronic Data Manager)

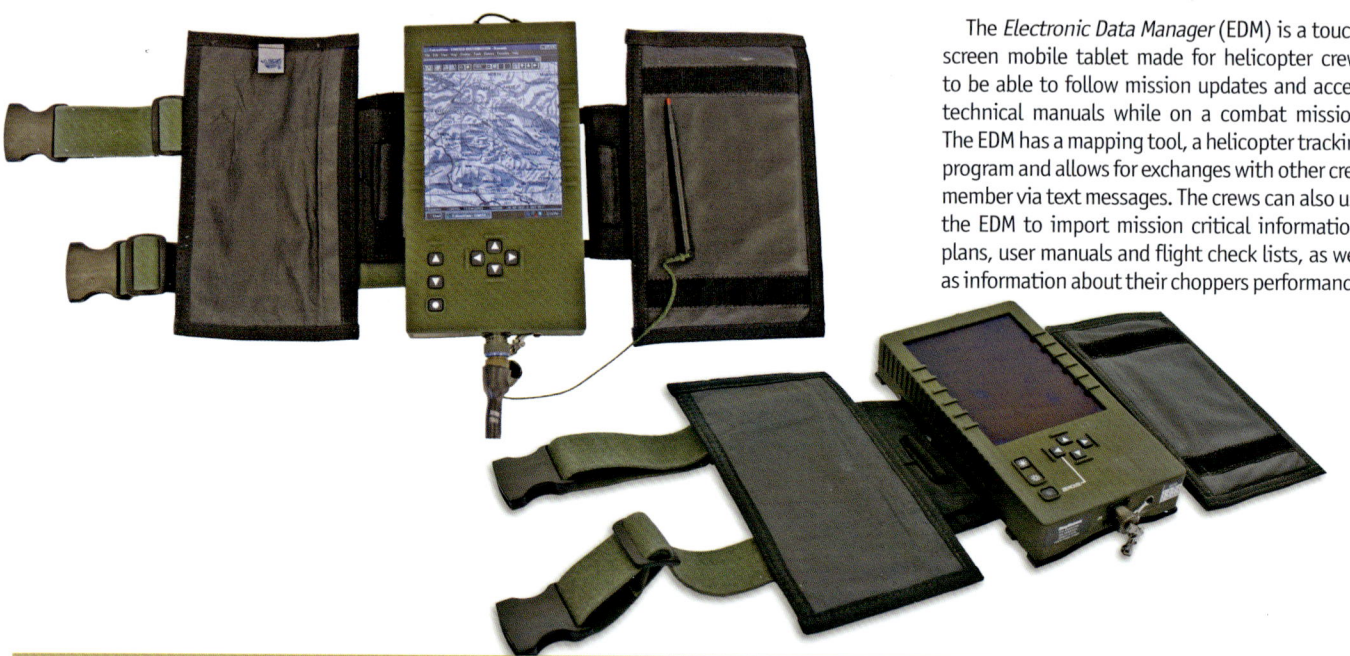

The *Electronic Data Manager* (EDM) is a touch-screen mobile tablet made for helicopter crews to be able to follow mission updates and access technical manuals while on a combat mission. The EDM has a mapping tool, a helicopter tracking program and allows for exchanges with other crew member via text messages. The crews can also use the EDM to import mission critical information, plans, user manuals and flight check lists, as well as information about their choppers performance.

The EAWIS wireless intercom system
(Encrypted Aircraft Wireless Intercom System)

The *Encrypted Aircraft Wireless Intercom System* is a now new helicopter intercom system design to upgrade communications inside US Army helicopters by bypassing the restrictions bound to the old wired intercoms. This allows for better communication inside the aircraft at all times, and better communication with the outside crew when maneuvering or refueling, by keeping outside personnel on the helicopters intercom.

The system is encrypted (NSA Type 1) and allows for up to 6 individuals at any given time.

the CEP et CEPS active ear protection

(Communication Ear Plugs and Communication Enhancement and Protection System)

The *Communication Ear Plugs* (CEP) are an active intra-auricular audio system mounted inside the HGU-56 helmet and provide a connection to the communication system as well as sound dampening capabilities (on top of those of the helmet). This allows for the communication between the crew not to be degraded by ambient noise. The *Communication* *Enhancement and Protection System* (CEPS) is a set of microphones providing active reduction when the crew is in the ground. The CEPS will transmit voices and ambient noises while blocking combat sounds (detonations, helicopter sounds and so on). With the CEP and CEPS, the soldier has the ability to hear his surroundings without the harmful noises.

The MSS communication and information system

(Mounted Soldier System)

The *Mounted Solider System* is a modernization program ran as an upgrade for all mounted personnel (IFV and MBT crews). The MSS is built around a heads-up display for the CVCH helmet (Helmet Mounted Display Capabilities) and a wireless intercom (Cordless Communication Capabilities) for greater freedom of movement inside the vehicles. The MSS also integrates a cooling system to the crew's flak jackets *(Microclimate Cooling System)* and a series of purpose-built protections: CVCH, FREE and fireproof uniforms *(Soldier Force Protection System Capabilities)*.

The AIR WARRIOR Program

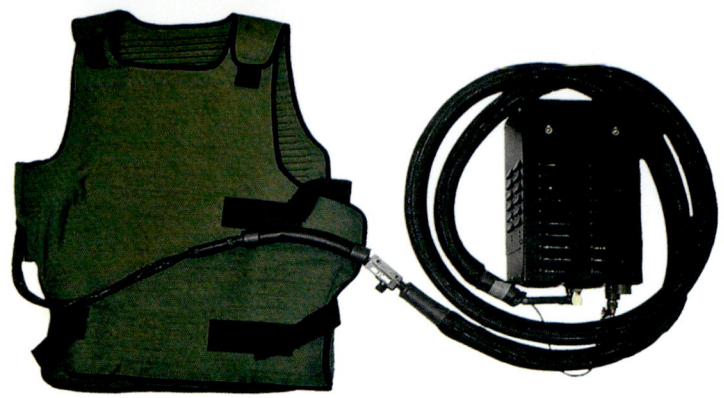

The *Air Warrior* aims at modernizing and upgrading the whole of the helicopter crew's equipment in the US Army. Air warrior has a rational, no-nonsense approach and integrates a number of sub systems aimed at completing each other. Those are the following:

- A2CU uniforms and ballistic protections

- Survival Equipment Subsystem : first aid, survival in hostile environment, communications and life jacket

- Microclimate Cooling System, a personal cooling system worn under the flak jacket

- Aircrew Integrated Helmet System HGU-56/P Electronic Data Manager

- Encrypted Aircraft Wireless System

- SKRAM bag

- CEP and CEPS system on the HGU-56/P

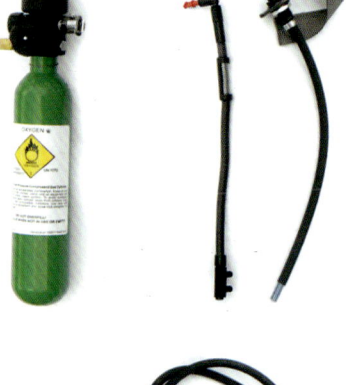

The LAND WARRIOR Program

Originaly developed during the *Cold War*, the Land Warrior is a host of systems designed to augment ground combat capacities for foot soldiers. The Land Warrior allows the individual soldier access to critical mission information about his location, the combat situation, available support and friendly troops positions.

The *Land warrior* is currently in action in Afghanistan with the 2nd *Stryker Cavalry Regiment*.

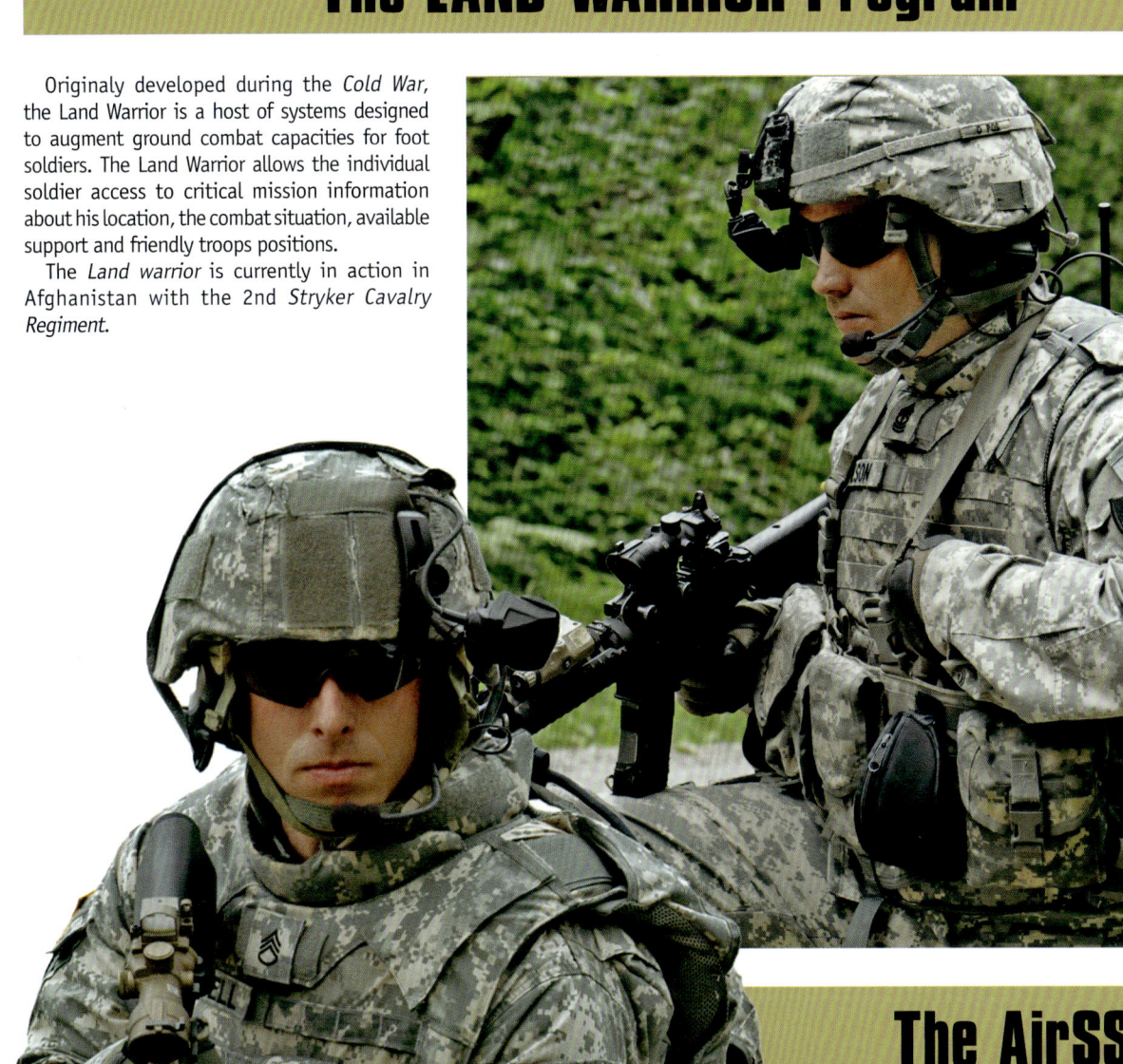

The AirSS Program
(Air Soldier System)

L'*Air Soldier System* (AirSS) est un système basé sur l'*Air Warrior*, destiné à donner une meilleure mobilité aux personnels de soute des voilures tournantes dans l'US Army, en allégeant leur équipement.

The NETT WARRIOR Program

The *NETT Warrior* is an integration of the soldier inside the global electronic battlefield. Based on 10 years of conflict and the lessons from the Land Warrior, the NETT WARRIOR has the goal of augmenting situation awareness at the soldier's level. Each soldier is provided with a tablet PC allowing him to check in real time all mission-critical information on the battlefield network: friendly and enemy positions, location of his unit, combat map, targets and mission objectives, enemy strongholds, available support and position of targets tagged for air support.

NETT WARRIOR aims at an optimization of the XXIst century US Army foot soldier.

Directed by Eric Micheletti.
Design and layout Magali Masselin.
Translation by Aurélien Morel.
Photos : DOD, US Army and ISAF.

ISBN: 978-2-35250-259-3
Publisher's number: 35250
© Histoire & Collections 2012

SA au capital de 182 938,82 €
5, avenue de la République
F-75541 Paris Cédex 11
FRANCE
www.histoireetcollections.com
Tel : +33-1 40 21 18 20 / Fax : +33-1 47 00 51 11

This book has been designed, typed, laid-out
and processed by Histoire & Collections on fully
integrated computer equipment.

Color separation: Studio A & C
Print by Calidad Graficas,
Spain, European Union,
October 2012